INTRODUCTION

Too often, customer needs, behaviors, and evolving expectations are overlooked in business decisions. Yet, companies that align themselves with their customers' desires, solve their pain points, and innovate with the end user in mind consistently demonstrate resilience and growth over the long term. The closer we get to understanding the individuals who drive demand, the better positioned we are to make successful business decisions.

This book brings together 100 powerful quotes that emphasize the value of taking a customer-centric approach. These words of wisdom come from industry leaders, successful investors, business strategists, and authors who have recognized the vital link between customer insight and business success. By exploring these quotes, you'll gain new perspectives on how adopting a customer-first mindset can drive better business decisions.

Dive in and get inspired!

100 QUOTES
ON
CUSTOMER
LOYALTY

STRATEGY LEADERSHIP COLLECTION

"Our take on competition boils down to one principle: We compete by focusing on our customer rather than the competition."

—R. David Thomas
Founder Wendy's

"There is only one boss – the customer. And he can fire everybody in the company from the chairman on down, simply by spending his money somewhere else."

—Sam Walton
Founder Walmart

"It is not the employer who pays the wages. Employers only handle the money. It's the customer who pays the wages."

—Henry Ford
Founder Ford Motor Company

"The purpose of a business is to create a customer who creates customers."

—Shiv Singh
Author

"Make a customer, not a sale."

—Katherine Barchetti
Founder K. Barchetti Shops

5

"The well-satisfied customer will bring the repeat sale that counts.

—James Cash Penney
Founder JCPenney

"Every company's greatest asset are its customers, because without customers there is no company."

—Michael LeBoeuf
Author

"Profit in business comes from repeat customers, customers that boast about your project or service, and that bring friends with them."

—W. Edwards Deming
Author

8

"Make a customer-obsessed revolution. Routinely look at the smallest nuance of the tiniest program through the customer's eyes – that is, as the customer perceives it, not you."

—Tom Peters
Author

9

"The result of a business is a satisfied customer."

—Peter Drucker
Author

"If we start to focus on ourselves, instead of focusing on our customers, that will be the beginning of the end ... We have to try and delay that day for as long as possible."

—Jeff Bezos
Founder Amazon

Smart companies have realized that customer loyalty is the most powerful sales and marketing tool they have."

—Bill Price
Investor

12

"A company's value isn't found in spreadsheets or accounting records but in the hearts and wallets of customers."

—Patrick Wierckx
Author

13

"I think the only way to maintain profitability is to meet the needs of the customers."

—Ofra Strauss
Chairperson Strauss Group

"Your customers are the lifeblood of your business. Their needs and wants impact every aspect of your business, from product development to content marketing to sales to customer service."

—John Rampton
Entrepreneur

15

"The magic formula that successful businesses have discovered is to treat customers like guests and employees like people."

—Tom Peters
Author

"In the business waltz, customers lead, and those who follow their cues will dance their way to financial success."

— Patrick Wierckx
Author

17

"A customer is the most important visitor on our premises, he is not dependent on us. We are dependent on him."

—Mahatma Ghandi
Lawyer

18

"We're not competitor obsessed; we're customer obsessed."

—Jeff Bezos
Founder Amazon

"We should no longer think about a company's market share or revenue growth as the measure of its success; the true measure of its strength lies in its ability to keep its customers coming back—its customer loyalty."

—Patrick Wierckx
Author

"A satisfied customer is one who will continue to buy from you, seldom shop around, refer other customers and in general be a superstar advocate for your business."

— Gregory Ciotti
Marketing Consultant

"Competitive advantages can only be valuable if they benefit customers."

—Patrick Wierckx
Author

"Our greatest asset is the customer! Treat each customer as if they are the only one!"

— **Laurice Leitao**
Customer Service Professional

"One customer, well taken care of, could be more valuable than the 10,000$ worth of advertising."

—Jim Rohn
Entrepreneur

"Rival companies can battle for market dominance, but customer spending is what matters."

— Patrick Wierckx
Author

25

"If we don't take care of our customers, someone else will."

—Edgar Mitchell
Astronaut

"The best advertising is done by satisfied customers."

—Philip Kotler
Author

27

"The true value of any competitive advantage hinges on having a customer advantage."

—Patrick Wierckx
Author

"To understand the customer, walk a day in their shoes."

—Japanese Proverb

29

"Customer first will last."

—Unknown

30

"Customer satisfaction is worthless. Customer loyalty is priceless."

—Jeffrey Gitomer
Author

31

"Customers wield the ultimate power; their choices shape a company's ultimate success or failure."

—Patrick Wierckx
Author

"(Customer) Satisfaction is a rating. (Customer) loyalty a brand."

—Shep Hyken
Author

33

"The purpose of a business is to create a customer."

—Peter Drucker
Author

"Loyal customers, they don't just come back, they don't simply recommend you, they insist that their friends do business with you."

—Chip Bell
Author

35

"The most important single thing is to focus obsessively on the customer."

—Jeff Bezos
Founder Amazon

"Once you create a loyal customer base, it's tough for a competitor to take that away."

—Joseph D. Mansueto
Entrepreneur

37

"The purpose of a business is to create and keep a customer."

—Peter Drucker
Author

38

"The customer, in spirit and in flesh, must pervade the organization – every system in every department, every procedure, every measure, every meeting, every decision."

—Tom Peters
Author

39

"Don't fight your competitors, love your customers."

—Patrick Wierckx
Author

40

"Generally accepted accounting principles actually hide the value of a loyal customer, an impressive feat of concealment given what loyalty can do for the great majority of companies."

—Fred Reichheld
Author

"Many companies still cling to the outdated belief that customers are swayed by low prices or high product quality alone. By failing to recognize the crucial role of loyal customers, they run the risk of losing their hard-earned competitive advantages in rapidly changing markets"

—Patrick Wierckx
Author

"The bond (or not!) between customers and companies is one of the most important factors in determining long-term business success."

—Nick Sleep
Investor

"Investors are eager to crunch numbers and analyze companies from various angles, but they forget to put themselves in the shoes of the people who truly matter—the customers."

—Patrick Wierckx
Author

"Focusing on the customer makes a company more resilient."

—Jeff Bezos
Founder Amazon

"By adopting a customer perspective, investors can evolve into individuals who view volatility as an opportunity rather than a source of fear."

—Patrick Wierckx
Author

"Exceptional customer experiences are the only sustainable platform for competitive differentiation."

—Kerry Bodine
Author

47

"The customer is the final inspector."

—Steve Jobs
Entrepreneur

"For most companies to thrive over the long-term, one constituency must be looked after before all others and, contrary to what some on Wall Street or in Westminster may suggest, that constituency is the customer."

—Nick Sleep
Investor

49

"Success comes from listening to your customer."

—Richard Branson
Entrepreneur

"Our focus is on the customers. We believe that if we do that well, competition, prices and profits will all take care of themselves."

—Bhavish Aggarwal
Entrepreneur

"We must recognize that behind every profit statement lies the tale of customer choice, and those who grasp this concept discover the key to success."

—Patrick Wierckx
Author

52

"It is a company's customers who effectively control what it can and cannot do."

—Clayton Christensen
Author

"Don't just satisfy your customers, delight them. Anybody who has happy customers is likely to have a pretty good future."

—Warren Buffett
Investor

"If you don't care, your customer never will."

—Marlene Blaszcyk
Founder MotivateUs.com

"Those who view businesses from a competitive perspective often miss the crucial point that cash flows are driven by the behavior of a company's existing and future customers, not by its competitors."

—Patrick Wierckx
Author

"It is not your customer's job to remember you, it is your obligation and responsibility to make sure they don't have the chance to forget you."

—Patricia Fripp
Author

"Rule 1: The customer is always right. Rule 2: If the customer is ever wrong, read Rule 1."

—Stew Leonard
Founder Stew Leonard's

"The golden rule for every businessman is put yourself in your customer's place."

—Orison Swett Marden
Author

"The heartbeat of any business is the rhythm of customer transactions, each beat echoing the financial vitality of the company."

— Patrick Wierckx
Author

60

"If you make a sale, you can make a living. If you make an investment of time and good service in a customer, you can make a fortune."

—Jim Rohn
Entrepreneur

"When the customer comes first,
the customer will last."

—Robert Half
Founder

"To succeed in business, put the interest of the customer ahead of your own."

—James Cook
Author

63

"Behind every profit margin lies the silent applause of satisfied customers."

— Patrick Wierckx
Author

"The customer's perception is your reality."

— Kate Zabriskie
Entrepreneur

"If the end result is customer satisfaction, your business will thrive. If the end result is customer loyalty, your business will bloom."

— Pooja Agnihotri
Author

"For investors, the compass pointing to sustained wealth is not in quarterly reports alone but in the perpetual loyalty of customers."

— Patrick Wierckx
Author

"Customer service should not be a department. It should be the entire company."

— Tony Hsieh
Entrepreneur

"Your customers are responsible for your company's reason for existing."

— **Marilyn Suttle**
Author

"There is a big difference between a satisfied customer and a loyal customer. Never settle for 'satisfied'."

— Shep Hyken
Author

"Since the only way a business can retain customer loyalty is by delivering superior value, high loyalty is a certain sign of solid value creation."

— Fred Reichheld
Author

"Financial metrics reveal past success, but customer loyalty reveals its sustainability."

— Patrick Wierckx
Author

"Every day we're saying, 'How can we keep this customer happy?' How can we get ahead in innovation by doing this, because if we don't, somebody else will."

— Bill Gates
Entrepreneur

"Few businesses think of customers as annuities."

— Fred Reichheld
Author

74

"Be dramatically willing to focus on the customer at all costs, even at the cost of obsoleting your own stuff."

— Scott Cook
Co-Founder Intuit

"Your most unhappy customers are your greatest source of learning."

— Bill Gates
Founder Microsoft

"The most important adage and the only adage is, the customer comes first, whatever the business, the customer comes first."

— **Kerry Stokes**
Chairman Seven Networks

"The stock market is a marketplace of promises, and the most reliable pledge is a company's commitment to meeting customer needs."

— Patrick Wierckx
Author

"Don't be focused on our competitor because they won't send us any money . . . the response to any crisis is to stay focused on the customer."

— Jeff Bezos
Founder Amazon

"Companies that focus on their stock price will eventually lose their customers. Companies that focus on their customers will eventually boost their stock price. This is simple but forgotten by countless managers."

— Morgan Housel
Author

80

"A company's cash flow originates from the loyalty of its customers. Those who grasp this connection secure the foundation of future success."

— Patrick Wierckx
Author

"A customer's journey doesn't end at the point of purchase. True success lies in fostering long-term relationships and building that forever transaction."

— Robbie Kellman Baxter
Author

"When we look at our customer, we don't see the lady with $100 worth of groceries; we see the $52,000 she might spend with us over the next ten years and profit she'll bring to our business. That profit is our reward for listening to our customers."

— Stew Leonard
Founder Stew Leonard's

"Customer service shouldn't just be a department; it should be the entire company."

— Tony Hsieh
Former CEO Zappos

"If you work just for money, you'll never make it, but if you love what you're doing and you always put the customer first, success will be yours."

— Ray Kroc
Founder McDonald's

"Repeat customers are the quickest way to build a solid business."

— Jack Taylor
Founder Enterprise-Rent-A-Car

"Competitive threats may be loud, but customer cash flows speak louder. Companies should prioritize understanding customer preferences over responding to every competitive move."

— Patrick Wierckx
Author

"It's not enough to have your customer-facing teams focused on the customers — you need to have the whole organization on board."

— Jovana Kandic
VP Customer Experience

"The lifeline of every successful company is woven from threads of customer trust and loyalty."

— Patrick Wierckx
Author

"Your customers are not you. They don't look like you, they don't think like you, they don't do the things that you do, they don't have your expectations or assumptions. If they did, they wouldn't be your customers; they'd be your competitors."

— Mike Kuniasvsky
Author

"Profitability is the echo of customer satisfaction; wise investors know that the applause of a delighted customer base resounds far louder than quarterly earnings reports."

— Patrick Wierckx
Author

"Know what your customers want most and what your company does best. Focus on where those two meet."

— Kevin Stirtz
Author

"A company's strategy may sound compelling, but what validates it is its customer adoption."

— Patrick Wierckx
Author

"Your customer doesn't care how much you know until they know how much you care."

— Damon Richards
Customer Care Expert

"Behind every flourishing business stands a legion of satisfied customers, the true architects of sustainable cash flow."

— Patrick Wierckx
Author

"It never ceases to amaze me that companies spend millions to attract new customers (people they don't know) and spend next to nothing to keep the ones they've got! Seems to me the budgets should be reversed!"

— Tom Peters
Author

"In the grand equation of business, customers are the variables that determine the outcome; for organizations, mastering this equation unlocks their true potential."

— Patrick Wierckx
Author

"We see our customers as invited guests to a party, and we are the hosts. It's our job every day to make every important aspect of the customer experience a little bit better."

— Jeff Bezos
Founder Amazon

"It is exceptionally difficult to build and sustain a competitive advantage rooted entirely in price, selection, or even quality. But it is entirely possible for a business to be the best in its category at how it makes customers feel."

— Jay Baer
Author

"Customers are the currency of success, wielding the power to elevate or diminish a company's financial stature."

— Patrick Wierckx
Author

100

- The End -

www.ingramcontent.com/pod-product-compliance
Lightning Source LLC
Chambersburg PA
CBHW071101240526
45471CB00016B/2302